CHRISTIAN VERSE

Ryan Doherty

ARTHUR H. STOCKWELL LTD.
Torrs Park   Ilfracombe   Devon
Established 1898
www.ahstockwell.co.uk

British Library Cataloguing-in-Publication Data.
A catalogue record for this book is available
from the British Library.

ISBN 0 7223 3689-6
Printed in Great Britain by
Arthur H. Stockwell Ltd.
Torrs Park   Ilfracombe
Devon

Contents

Jesus' Lot

O Lord, you have given us your lot,
Love, joy, peace, patience, kindness;
You have given us power by giving us your sacraments
Of your most holy blood in the Eucharist;
Bless us, O Lord.

You have shown us miracles to be thankful of;
Heal us, O Lord.
You have given us your music of psalms and hymns,
O Lord, you hear us and we hear you;
Bless us, O Lord.

You have given us your gospel of word and action
To imitate;
You have given us your heaven and earth
To reward us;
Bless us, O Lord.

You have given us eternal life.
In happiness, O Lord,
You have forgiven us our sins;
Teach us, O Lord;
Bless us, O Lord.

You have given us your saints and Holy Spirit
To inspire us;
You have given us your priests and bishops
To guide us;
Bless us, O Lord.

You have given us your Church
To build faith in us;
We are your people of God;
In giving us our daily needs,
O Lord, you have truly blessed us.

The Church

In the church
We see the apostles as cardinals.
In the church
We see the saints as witnesses.

In the church
We see our heavenly dwelling.
In the church
We see our prayers answered.

In the church
We receive the gifts of the Holy Spirit.
In the church
The nations become one.

In the church
We are taught.
In the church
We are forgiven.

In the church
We see the economy of works.
In the church
We see the charity of the needy.

In the church
We see marriage as love.
In the church
We see happiness and peace.

God

God, you are the creator of heaven and earth;
God, you are light in darkness;
God, you are visible and invisible;
God, you are natural and supernatural;
God, you are spiritual and transcendent;
God, you are power and glory;
God, you are the revealer;
God, you are symbolic;
God, you are eternal;
God, you are peace;
God, you are beautiful;
God, you are love;
God, you are one;
God, you are everything good.

Jesus

You are the Christ;
You are the Messiah;
You are the anointed one;
You are the Son of God;
You are the holy one;
You are the suffering servant;
You are the prince of peace;
You are the Lord;
You are our song;
You are our king;
You are our helper;
You are our Saviour;
You are love;
You are God.

The Old Testament

Book of the law and the prophets;
Book of faith and hope;
Book of wisdom and understanding;
Book of creation and revelation;
Book of theophanies and prayers;
Book of song and praise;
Book of Abraham and progeny;
Book of Noah and Moses;
Book of King David and the psalms;
Book of the Covenant and Israel;
Book of God and man.

The Sacraments

Baptism of enlightenment and grace;
Eucharist of food of immortality;
Penance of intercession and forgiveness;
Confirmation of anointing and seal;
Holy orders of priestly, prophetic and kingly office;
Marriage of love and happiness;
Anointing of the sick of prayers and gratitude.

Jesus' Kindled Love

I'm sitting here pondering
If I am going to be;
I'm sitting here wondering
If it will come to me.

His words they never leave me,
I'm wondering where to go;
This kindled love that leads me
To places I don't know.

This kindled love that feeds me,
I hope it starts to grow.

Holy Spirit

You are the spirit of cloud and light;
You are the spirit of fire and water;
You are the spirit of tongues;
You are the spirit of anointing and seal of approval;
You are the consoler;
You are divine;
You are the spirit of the apostles;
You are the spirit of life;
You are the spirit of promise;
You are the spirit of glory;
You are the spirit of truth;
You are the spirit of the prophets;
You are the spirit of Christ;
You are the spirit of the gospel;
You are the spirit of God.

God's Treasure

God, your treasure is freedom of spirit;
God, your treasure is friendship;
God, your treasure is love;
God, your treasure is a gift of a child;
God, your treasure is peace;
God, your treasure is worship;
God, your treasure is music;
God, your treasure is charity;
God, your treasure is happiness and eternity;
God, your treasure is your word;
God, your treasure is creation and the heavens;
God, your treasure is man and woman;
God, your treasure is the saints;
God, your treasure is your son, Jesus.

Love

Love is marriage;
Love is someone you can hold on to;
Love is making people smile and laugh;
Love is where we belong;
Love is a blessing;
Love is goodness;
Love is faith and hope;
Love is prayer;
Love is creation;
Love is friendship;
Love is helping the poor and sick;
Love is kindness;
Love is joy and happiness;
Love is patience;
Love is eternal;
Love is God.

God's People

God's people are a chosen race;
God's people are a royal priesthood;
God's people are a messianic people;
God's people are a holy nation;
God's people are the baptised;
God's people are a sure seed of unity;
God's people are a people of song;
God's people are the poor and sinners;
God's people are the sick;
God's people are the faithful laity;
God's people are compassionate;
God's people are spiritual and free;
God's people are a temple of the Holy Spirit;
God's people are Jesus' brothers and sisters;
God's people are sons and daughters of God;
God's people are happy and eternal;
God's people are love.

Heaven

Heaven is the place of life;
Heaven is the home of us all;
Heaven is the place of light;
Heaven is the place of the messianic banquet;
Heaven is the place of the heavenly Jerusalem;
Heaven is God the Father's house;
Heaven is the great wedding feast;
Heaven is paradise;
Heaven is the place of joy and happiness;
Heaven is the place where no ear has heard of;
Heaven is the place where no eyes have seen;
Heaven is the place where no heart has conceived;
Heaven is eternity.